HEAT AND COLD

(Original French title:
Le chaud et le froid)

by
Jean-Pierre Maury

Translated from the French by
Albert V. Carozzi and Marguerite Carozzi

BARRON'S

New York • London • Toronto • Sydney

First English Language edition published in 1989 by
Barron's Educational Series, Inc.

© 1987 Hachette/Fondation Diderot-La Nouvelle Encyclopédie, Paris, France.

The title of the French edition is *Le chaud et le froid*

All inquiries should be addressed to:
Barron's Educational Series, Inc.
250 Wireless Boulevard
Hauppauge, NY 11788

International Standard Book No. 0-8120-4211-5

Library of Congress Catalog Card No. 89-6722

Library of Congress Cataloging-in-Publication Data

Maury, Jean-Pierre.
    [Le chaud et le froid. English]
    Heat and cold / by Jean-Pierre Maury ; translated from the French by
    Albert V. Carozzi and Marguerite Carozzi. — 1st English language ed.
    p.   cm. — (Barron's focus on science)
    Translation of: Le chaud et le froid.
    Includes index.
    ISBN 0-8120-4211-5
    1. Heat—Juvenile literature.   2. Cold—Juvenile literature.
    I. Title.   II. Series.
QC256.M3813   1989
536—dc20   89-6722
                                                    CIP

PRINTED IN FRANCE

901   9687   987654321

TABLE OF CONTENTS

Heat   4

The Advantages of a Thermometer   4
Zero to Hundred Degrees Celsius   7
What Is Heat?   8
The Advantage of Wooden Spoons   10
What Makes Smoke Rise?   11
The Hot-Air Balloon   12
Why Are Flames Pointed?   14
Clothes That Keep Us Warm   16

Radiation   18

Which Objects Radiate?   20
All Objects Radiate   22
The Light of a Lamp   24
Taking the Temperature of a Volcano   24
The Mirror, the Windowpane, and Black Velvet   28
The Thermos Bottle   30
The Hothouse   32
Cool Clear Nights   32

Water, Ice, and Vapor   36

The Effect of Heat   38
Why Does Water Evaporate?   40
The Bowl and the Carafe   42
The Plume of the Teakettle   44
Why Is Our Breath Visible in Cold Weather?   46
Steam   48
Morning Dew   49
Why Does Alcohol Cool the Skin?   49
The Cooling of Water   50

Animal Heat   52

What Causes Animal Heat?   54
Dry Heat, Humid Heat   58
Why Are There No Mice the Size of a Fly?   59
The Large Ears of Elephants   60
How to Keep Warm in Icy Waters   61
The Cold That Makes You Blush   62

Heat and Humanity   64

An Astonishing Solution: the Igloo   66
In a Hot and Dry Area   69
The Sun Is the Origin of Everything   70
Solar Energy   73
A Marvelous Invention: the Tree   74

Index   76

Heat

Heat is a sensation: "It's hot," "It's too hot," "It burns." However, we do not stop there but ask questions: Why does the soup cool? And why does it cool faster if one blows on it? Why is a melting ice cube capable of cooling a large glass of water?

To answer all these questions, it is necessary to know what we are talking about. Hence, our sensation of "hot" and "hotter" must be improved: it is necessary to invent the thermometer.

If I place my hand in a bowl of water, I can tell whether the water is very cold, cold, lukewarm, warm, or hot.

However, if I test another bowl the following day, I cannot tell if the water is exactly as warm as the first one. Furthermore, what I call "hot" may perhaps be only "warm" for somebody else (this often happens at the dinner table when those who think that the food is "too hot" must wait longer than the others).

The Advantages of a Thermometer

To arrive at a general agreement so that everybody could test the temperature of a body in the same fashion, in different places, and at different times, instruments called thermometers were invented. When dipping a thermometer in water, one can read a number, which is the temperature of the water. For instance, if it reads 95, we say that the temperature of the water is ninety-five degrees

5

To compare the temperature of a lake in the Alps . . .

Celsius (and one writes 95°C).

This is certainly much better than testing with a finger or hand for several reasons:

First, hot water flowing from different faucets, which I find "burning hot," may have different temperatures, such as 122, 129, or 140, that the thermometer can tell with precision. This may be compared to a watch that tells the exact time instead of merely my saying that it is "late" or "very late" according to whether I am hungry or tired.

Second advantage: if I test the water again a month later (or ten years later), the thermometer will indicate if the water is exactly as hot as the first time.

Third advantage: if I want to compare the temperature of two very distant objects, such as a lake in the Alps and one in Japan, I can do it by writing letters to a Japanese and a Swiss friend. With their thermometers, they can test the temperature of their respective lakes and send me a reply. Such a comparison would hardly be

. . . with that of a lake in Japan, thermometers are necessary.

possible otherwise.

Finally, special thermometers read very high temperatures, such as that of red-hot iron or a pile of embers that nobody would dare to touch with the hand!

Zero to Hundred Degrees Celsius

The most commonly used thermometers are minute bottles with a very long and thin neck. Inside is a liquid (often red or silvery) that rises with increas-ing temperature. To complete the construction of the thermometer one has merely to inscribe numbers on the neck that indicate temperature. Nevertheless, one should make sure that two different thermometers dipped in the same liquid always indicate the same temperature. This is how it is done.

A container is filled with small pieces of ice, which begin to melt. If the thermometer is dipped into this mixture of ice and water, the liquid of the thermometer stops at a certain point on the neck. One may start all over again as often as one wishes, or change location, change the container, or change the ice: the liquid of the thermometer always stops at the same place. This means that the melting ice is always at the same temperature. A little over two hundred years ago, it was decided to call this temperature "zero degree." A line is inscribed on the neck of the thermometer at the place where the liquid stops when the thermometer is dipped into melting ice. Facing this line is written 0°C (32°F).

In the same way, but taking greater care, one finds that boiling water in an area close to sea level is always at the same temperature, which one decides to call a "hundred degrees C."

Thus the marks 0°C (32°F) and 100°C (212°F) are inscribed on the neck of the thermometer, and the interval between the two marks is divided into a hundred equal parts. Thus we have all the temperatures between 0 and 100°C.

Other thermometers are not divided between 0 and 100°C. For instance, Daniel Gabriel Fahrenheit, lacking other references, decided that 0°F was the lowest winter temperature observed in Dantzig, Germany, which is equivalent to −17.8°C, and hence 100°F equals 37.7°C.

What Is Heat?

If I pour a cup of hot coffee into a cold cup, after one minute the coffee is less hot and the cup is no longer cold. Some "thing" has passed from the coffee to the cup. This "thing" is heat.

Similarly, an object that appears hot to me (to know this I have to either touch it or at least get closer to it) is an object that produces heat: if I place my hand in hot water, heat leaves the water and passes into my hand.

An object that appears cold to me is an object that takes away heat: if I place my hand in cold water, heat passes from my hand into the water.

Warning! "Temperature" and "heat" are often confused. For example, one says, "heat is unbearable!" instead of "temperature is unbearable!" (perhaps because it is easier to say). However, we must remember that heat is something that *passes from one object to another* (for instance from the coffee to the cup), whereas temperature belongs to one object alone.

One can say that the cup has a temperature of 40°C (104°F), just as one can say that an object is 1 meter (3 feet) high. However, the "heat of the cup" means nothing.

The Advantage of Wooden Spoons

Heat travels inside an object from a hot place to a cold one. If one leaves a metal spoon in a pot of boiling water, the end of the spoon that sticks out soon becomes very hot and if you touch it, you are burnt.

Nevertheless, heat does not travel as easily inside all materials. If one touches a wooden spoon, one is not burnt at all.

The two ends of a wooden spoon can remain at very different temperatures for a long time because heat has difficulty traveling through wood. When a material does not let heat get through easily, it is said to be "insulating." Hence wood is a good insulator. In contrast, iron is a good conductor of heat, as are all metals.

Therefore, to avoid being burnt, wooden spoons are made and wooden handles are put on pots and pans (or sometimes plastic ones: plastic is also a good insulator). Similarly, many houses in cold climates are built of wood. Of course, wood is very plentiful in these places and therefore not very

With a wooden spoon, *one is never burnt.*

expensive. But, above all, wood is a good insulator that prevents heat from leaving the house too easily.

One may also learn in another way that wood is an insulator and metal a conductor of heat, namely by merely touching a piece of wood and a piece of metal that lie outside side by side in wintertime: metal seems much colder than wood. Nevertheless, if they have been in the same place for a long time, they must surely have the same temperature. Why the difference?

When your hand touches cold metal, heat passes from your hand to the metal. In this metal, heat circulates very rapidly and spreads evenly all over it. Thus, although the temperature of the entire metal rises a wee bit, the part resting against the hand does not become warmer than the rest: it continues to take heat from your hand, and hence it still seems very cold.

In contrast, heat that travels from your hand to a piece of wood cannot spread inside it because wood insulates. Heat does not reach beyond the very thin layer of wood resting against your hand. Temperature rises rapidly in this layer,

whereas the rest of the wood becomes hardly any warmer. After a short time, this thin layer reaches the same temperature as your hand; it ceases to take heat from your hand and hence wood does not feel colder.

This is the reason why one can touch pieces of wood scattered in the snow whereas touching a piece of very cold metal may be as painful as a burn.

What Makes Smoke Rise?

While burning, the tip of a stick produces hot gases and warms the surrounding air. Since hot air is lighter than cold air, it tends to rise as a cork does in water. If the air were a good conductor of heat, as metal is, heat would rapidly spread everywhere in the air of the room, there would be neither hot nor cold areas, and the air would not move.

However, air is a very poor conductor of heat and even more insulating than wood! Therefore, the air surrounding the tip of the stick becomes very hot and hence very light and rises rapidly in the cold air. It is immediately replaced by new cold air that heats rapidly in turn and rises, and so forth. Therefore, a stream of hot air is formed above the stick that rises straight up and carries along gases and dusts that form smoke.

This effect is of course also produced each time a fire is lit outdoors. The people who lived in America before the arrival of the Europeans used smoke to send signals from one hill to another. Shaking a hide, they either stopped the smoke or let it rise in gusts of variable size.

Thus they managed to convey messages.

The Hot Air Balloon

This was the first aircraft made by people to rise into the skies. It was called the Montgolfière because its inventors were the brothers Montgolfier, who first launched it in June 1783.

A hot-air balloon ends in a sort of chimney at its bottom. A fire is lit underneath this chimney: hot air rises into the balloon while the cold air in the balloon descends and becomes hot in turn so that the air inside the balloon is soon quite hot and hence lighter than the cold air surrounding it. The balloon thus tends to rise, and if it is sufficiently large and light, it is capable of lifting itself into the skies and carrying along weight, such as people.

This is how the first manned trip into the skies took place on October 21, 1783, from the Bois de Boulogne (a park in Paris) to Montrouge. A month earlier, a hot-air balloon carried three "passengers" of lesser weight: a lamb, a rooster, and a duck.

Since hydrogen (a gas lighter than air) was discovered at the same time, the hot-air balloon

was soon abandoned and replaced by balloons inflated with hydrogen. Nevertheless, the balloon is not a very good means of transportation because it is pushed randomly by the wind and cannot be efficiently controlled. Furthermore, the air cools in the hot-air balloon and it immediately descends unless there is enough fuel to keep the fire going underneath the chimney of the balloon so that the air that fills the balloon remains quite hot. All this increases the weight and hence the size of the balloon. To carry a person, a hot-air balloon must have a diameter of at least 10 meters.

Nevertheless, hot-air balloons have recently become fashionable again as a sport. Fans make their own balloons from a very fine fabric and use them for rides, carrying along bottles of propane to heat the air.

Why Are Flames Pointed?

Placing your hand on the side of a candle's flame, you can hardly feel the heat, even when your hand is quite close to the flame. However, if you place your hand above the flame, even at a certain distance, you will be burnt. Indeed, air heated by the flame rises straight up, whereas air on the flame's side is not hot at all, merely cool air that approaches the flame and is being warmed.

The flame itself, which is a mixture of burning gases and dusts, is carried by the ascending hot air current. The edges of this current are obviously less hot than the center; it is in the center where air rises most rapidly and carries the flame highest. This is why flames are always pointed. Sometimes, one even sees above a match or a candle a kind of flaming line that is quite long and rises straight up.

Therefore, a flame always produces heat right above it. For this reason, one must light firewood from underneath. One sets fire to a piece of paper underneath a pile of small pieces of wood and its rising flames heat the firewood until it begins to burn. If the piece of paper is put on top of the pile, the firewood is not heated and does not burn.

This is why smoke rises up the chimney instead of filling the room, and also why smoke does not rise very well right after the fire has been lit: the air in the

chimney is not yet warm and does not ascend. One must wait until it has heated enough that the system gets going and smoke does not spread in the room anymore. It is then said that the fire "draws well," that is, it draws the air from the room and sends it up the chimney, with its smoke.

Clothes That Keep Us Warm

Air is one of the best possible insulators. It would thus seem that the best way to keep warm in winter is to walk around completely naked. A piece of wood seems less cold than iron because the thin layer of air directly in contact with the skin warms up immediately but the heat does not spread into the surrounding air since it is a very poor conductor.

However, air is a gas that travels easily. Air warmed by our skin rises and is replaced by cold air, which in turn picks up heat from our skin and rises. Therefore, our skin continues to lose heat.

To avoid this, one must keep the air that has been warmed by our skin: this is the function of clothing! However, what "keeps warm" is not really cotton or wool, it is air trapped inside clothes (and if wool "keeps warm," it is because it traps a lot of air), or between

The most insulating clothes are those that trap lots of air.

16

layers of clothes (two light sweaters keep one warmer than a single heavy sweater because they trap more than one layer of air).

By the way, the warmest clothes are those that trap the most air: furs trap it between the

many individual hairs, and a down blanket, which is made of feathers contained between two layers of cloth, traps air between the barbs of the feathers. So much air is trapped in a down blanket that it is very light and inflated. Indeed, it consists of almost nothing but air, *air that cannot move*!

There is a better example of trapped air: Styrofoam, which is used for the packing of ice and fish. It is an extremely light material made of a great many bubbles glued together. Styrofoam is thus an excellent insulator and to understand that it is "nothing but holes," one needs only to feel its weight. The walls of the bubbles are very thin, and they serve merely to keep the enclosed air static. Therefore, air cannot escape and warm itself against the outside air and then return to cool, giving off heat to the ice that one wants to keep cold.

If we wear clothes, it is mainly to trap air. Of course, special clothes are used for other purposes: they are either rain or wind proof or they protect us against the desert sun. Some clothes serve merely to make us beautiful or elegant so as to attract attention.

Radiation

We have already learned about two ways of receiving heat: when heat passes through a conducting body that we are touching (such as a metal spoon immersed in hot water) or when heat is transported by a moving insulator like air (this heat is felt above the flame of a candle).

However, there is a third way to receive heat, in front of a fireplace for example. Something strange happens there: my back is freezing and my stomach is roasting.

I t is very easy to understand why my back is cold. Indeed, the fire draws upward (in the chimney) a mass of gas and hot air as does the flame of a candle. To replace this rising air, the surrounding air rushes toward the fire at a speed increasing with the size of the fire. Therefore, if I turn toward the fire, my back receives the onrushing cold air and is colder than it would be if I were not standing in front of a fire!

It is less easy to understand why my stomach is roasting. Indeed, this heat that I feel cannot come from either one of the two processes that we al-

Hot air rises in the chimney and cold air replaces it.

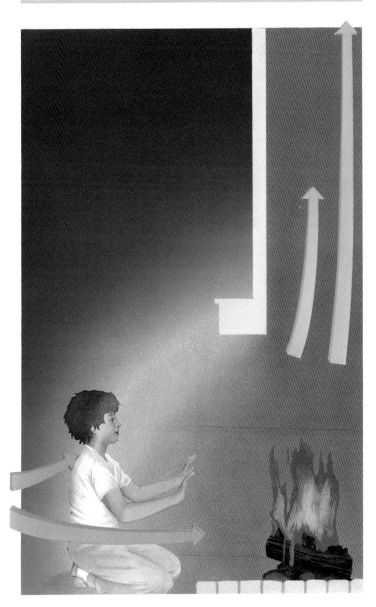

ready know because the air that surrounds me is cold.

There must be a third way to receive or give off heat. It is called radiation. It is through radiation that my stomach is roasting when I approach the fire and it is radiation that I feel on my skin when I face the sun. The fire and the sun send radiation: both are said to *radiate*.

Which Objects Radiate?

To this question, the answer is naturally: the sun, embers, an electric heater, and so on, objects that produce light. Indeed, we think about radiation, rays, and light, which is perfectly correct: light is radiation. When a cloud passes in front of the sun, suddenly we no longer feel its radiation on our faces. Similarly, if in front of the fireplace I hold a book in front of my face, it does not receive the light sent by the fire and heat is no longer felt. Thus very hot bodies radiate light, and the skin feels heat when receiving that light. However, this is not the end of it by far!

Let us imagine a piece of iron heated until it is "red-hot," that is, so hot that it produces red light as embers do. If I move my hand just a little toward this piece of iron, I feel the heat that it releases toward me exactly as embers do. I am sure that this heat is radiation since I can feel it just as well when I put my hand underneath that piece of iron. If it were hot air, I would feel it only above the iron because hot air rises.

Well, this is not astonishing because the piece of iron sends off red light, which means that it really radiates. But after some

The iron is still radiating even though it has turned gray again.

20

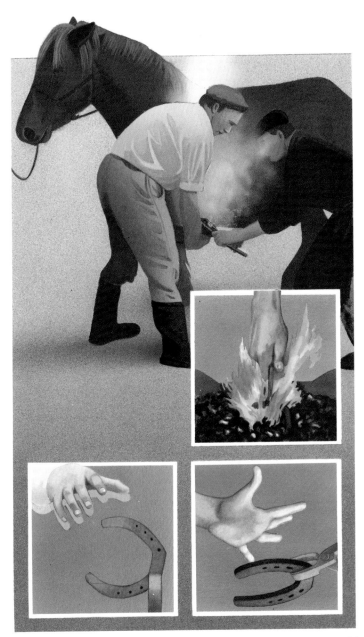

time, the iron cools (which is normal since it loses all the heat it radiates plus the heat taken away by air). Soon it is no longer red: it sends no more light. Nevertheless, if I move my hand closer, *I can still feel radiation*!

Thus, in addition to visible radiation (light), an invisible radiation exists that we can feel very well. This is called infrared radiation, or infrared.

Hence, luminous objects are not the only ones that radiate or send heat by radiation. In fact, all objects radiate.

All Objects Radiate

Very hot objects (red-hot iron, embers, and the sun) radiate simultaneously light (which is visible) and infrared (which is invisible). Objects that are not hot enough to send light radiate

only infrared. So does the piece of iron that is cooling and is no longer red. So does a pan that has been taken out of the oven but is still hot. So does my skin. So does a stick, a stone, a leaf of a tree! Indeed, so do all objects radiate!

However, when I touch a leaf of a tree, I do not feel heat because the leaf is colder than my hand. It radiates anyway, as does any other object. It sends infrared in all directions, in particular, toward my hand. However, my hand sends stronger radiations toward the leaf. In fact, when I touch the leaf, it is the leaf that "feels" the radiation of my hand. This does not mean that it does not radiate also, but merely that it radiates less than my hand, just as my hand radiates less—much less—than the red-hot iron radiates.

23

The Light of a Lamp

Every object without exception radiates invisible infrared. In order to radiate light in addition, it has to be very hot. The hotter the object, the brighter and whiter its light. Heated iron turns dark red, then light red, then orange, then a brighter and brighter yellow with increasing temperature.

Similarly, the flame of a candle sends us light because it contains very hot and burning gases and dusts. An even hotter flame, such as that of a kerosene lamp, produced stronger and whiter light.

There are flames that are even hotter, such as that of acetylene. The light produced by burning acetylene is a dazzling white. However, acetylene lamps have an unpleasant odor, are difficult to regulate, and may cause serious burns.

Without danger, an even higher temperature can be reached—and hence an even brighter light—by having an electric current flow through a metal wire enclosed in a glass bulb devoid of air (if air were present, the wire would burn). The electric current heats the wire, and since the temperature becomes very high, the wire radiates a strong white light.

This is how ordinary electric bulbs operate. Unfortunately, while radiating light, the wire also radiates much infrared, which is of no use for lighting since it is invisible. To avoid this waste, completely different systems have been invented (such as neon tubes) in which light is produced by another method without heating.

At any rate, the most important "lamp" for us, the sun, produces light because it is very hot. The temperature at its surface reaches about 6000°C (10,832°F)! Therefore, the sun sends us, in addition to an enormous quantity of infrared, an equally huge quantity of light.

Taking the Temperature of a Volcano

Very hot molten rock called lava is formed in active volcanoes. Cold lava is generally of a blackish-gray color, whereas very hot lava is as red as glowing embers.

It is important to know the temperature of lava to predict the activity of a volcano. For

this purpose, special thermometers are dipped into the lava, if one can approach closely enough. Otherwise other systems are used.

The color of lava changes according to its temperature just as the color of heated iron does. This variation in color allows us to estimate the temperature of the lava. For this purpose one looks through a tube containing a metal wire that stands out in black in front of the red background of the lava. An electric current is then sent through the wire to heat it. The wire turns red, and the current is increased steadily so that the metal becomes hotter and hotter and the red color lighter and lighter. At a certain moment, the wire is no longer visible: it "disappears"; that is, it has reached the same color as lava.

The same experiment was made earlier in front of an oven at various temperatures, and thus different shades of red, while checking each temperature of the oven for the required current that caused the wire to

"disappear."

When measuring the current that makes the wire disappear in front of the lava, one knows beforehand the temperature of the oven corresponding to that of this current: hence the lava has the same temperature. This is how the temperature of a volcano can be measured without getting burnt!

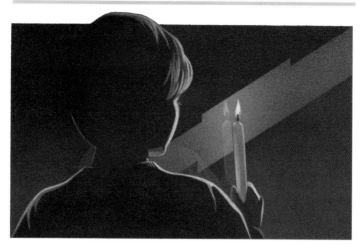

A flame is well reflected on a windowpane.

The Mirror, the Windowpane, and Black Velvet

What happens to radiation when it reaches an object? This radiation may be light or infrared or both. Let us first investigate what happens to light: this is easier because, at least, one can see what happens.

For instance, if I use a flashlight in a dark room, various things may happen depending on which object is lit up.

A mirror reflects the flashlight and may dazzle me if I am facing it.

I will see the reflection of the lamp on the windowpane and perhaps a tree branch lighted outside by my lamp. Indeed, part of the light is reflected toward me by the windowpane as by a mirror, whereas the other part of the light crosses the window and lights a branch.

Finally, if the light of the lamp falls on a dark material—for instance black velvet—I can hardly see anything. It is said that black velvet *absorbs* light (one might say as well that it swallows light).

Therefore, light hitting an object is split into three parts:

—one part is reflected;

—one part is absorbed (swallowed) by the object;

—one part passes through the object and continues to travel.

Depending upon the object,

these parts are of varying importance. The mirror, for instance, reflects almost all the light; it absorbs very little and does not let any part go through.

The windowpane reflects just a little bit and lets the greatest part go through (if it is a clear windowpane of good quality).

Black velvet reflects very little light and absorbs all the rest.

What occurs to infrared radiation hitting an object? The exact same thing happens: one part is reflected, one is absorbed, and the rest passes through the object. Therefore, when an object receives any radiation whatsoever (light or infrared), the only part of the radiation that serves to heat the body is the radiation that is absorbed. This seems evident if one thinks about it since the two other parts of radiation continue to travel! However, this gives strange results. For example, it is impossible to heat a mirror by radiation: it reflects practically everything it receives and absorbs very little.

Similarly, if one looks at two walls that are side by side in the sun, one white and the other dark, the white one dazzles the eyes because it reflects a great

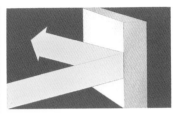

The mirror reflects almost all light received.

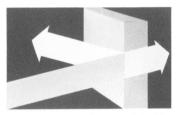

The windowpane reflects part of the light, absorbs some, and lets the rest pass through.

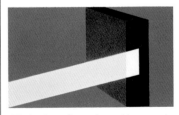

Black velvet reflects nothing and lets pass nothing: it absorbs all light.

part of the light received from the sun. This means that it absorbs less light than the dark wall (which receives the same amount and reflects almost nothing). Hence, the white wall heats less than the dark one. This is the reason walls are often painted white in hot countries, to prevent the overheating of houses by the sun. What could protect them even more than white paint? Mirrors! If houses were covered by mirrors, they would absorb no radiation at all. However, such covers would be very expensive, very fragile, and rather painful to the eyes of passers-by in the street who would be constantly dazzled by the light. It is better to use white paint.

The Thermos Bottle

This is a container that prevents the cooling of hot beverages or the heating of ice-cold

White houses reflect sunlight well and dazzle passers-by!

drinks. In both cases, one must avoid the passage of heat through the walls and for that purpose these walls must be good insulators.

The best insulator of all is a vacuum, that is, space without matter, not even air. In fact, without matter, heat cannot move around as in iron, nor can there be any disturbances or currents that carry heat as in the air.

Therefore, a thermos bottle has a double wall of very thin glass and between these two walls a vacuum is made (by pumping out the air before sealing the bottom). Thus, a "layer of vacuum" is obtained, and the only way heat can cross vacuum is by radiation: this is how solar radiation reaches the earth after crossing 150 million kilometers of vacuum (90 million miles).

For a thermos bottle to be efficient and keep coffee hot, for instance, radiation sent by the inner wall (heated by coffee) must be decreased as much as possible and absorbed by the outer wall. This is done by covering both walls with a thin layer of aluminum, which shines like a mirror. We have previously learned that this cover prevents the outer wall

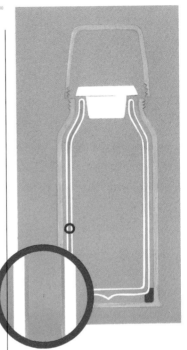

from absorbing radiation (a mirror absorbs practically nothing). Furthermore, this cover also prevents the inner wall from sending out any radiation! Indeed, a shiny object, like a mirror, radiates very little: much less than a dull and coarse object at the same temperature.

The inner wall of a thermos bottle therefore radiates very little (because it is shiny), and whatever small amount is radiated is reflected by the outer wall (because it is also shiny). Thus, there is almost no heat loss by radiation, and since heat can go through vacuum only by this means, the coffee remains very hot.

Of course, a thermos bottle is also capable of keeping drinks ice-cold because it is just as difficult for heat to enter as to leave!

The Hothouse

A house made entirely of glass, in which plants grow that normally live only in warmer climates, is called a hothouse. One can also grow "ordinary" plants there rather than in a garden. Why? Because in the hothouse plants are less cold at night.

Let us first understand why both garden plants and soil cool off at night since they are not in contact with a cold body nor is there anything cold in the neighborhood where the air might cool off. However, we have learned that all objects (stones, earth, and plants) radiate infrared. When they do so, they lose heat. During the day, the sun is there to provide them with as much heat as they lose and even more. However, at night, nothing gives them this

necessary heat and they cool (some plants may even freeze).

And in the hothouse? Why do plants not cool off there at night? They certainly radiate as much as plants in the open air, but the glass panes of the hothouse reflect back almost all the infrared that the plants radiate. Indeed, whereas a windowpane lets light go through, it reflects a great part of the infrared. Therefore, plants recover much of the heat they radiate and do not cool off as much as in the garden.

During the day, the panes prevent solar infrared radiation from reaching the plants, of course, but they let through the light that is the greatest part of solar radiation and that provides all the heat they need.

This is why the growth of plants is improved in a hothouse. Furthermore, a hothouse protects the plants from the wind and gives them a constant humidity. Its major role, however, is to prevent infrared from leaving.

Cool Clear Nights

Nights are cold because the earth, plants, and walls radiate infrared. Furthermore, the air

Plants radiate *as much in a garden as in a hothouse, but a hothouse reflects back a great part of their radiation.*

33

cools when touching plants, the ground, and the cold walls. When there are no clouds, all radiation toward the skies is lost. However, when a layer of clouds spreads over the land, the layer acts like the windowpanes of a hothouse: it reflects toward the ground part of the infrared sent by the ground and the plants. Thus, it is during clear nights that plants cool off

most, as do the ground and the stones. Therefore, nights are very cold in a desert where the air is very dry and where clouds almost never exist. In the Sahara Desert, it is very hot during the day but it is so cold at night that stones break into pieces (because the thin outer parts cool fast whereas the inside of the stone remains warm).

Water, Ice, and Vapor

Water, ice, and vapor have obviously something in common; when freezing, water turns into ice, and when boiling, it changes into vapor (all this plays an important role in the adventures of heat).

However, water, ice, and vapor are also very different:

—water is liquid, namely, it flows and takes on the shape of its container.

—ice is solid: a piece of ice has its own shape (a cube, for instance) and keeps it whether on a plate or in a glass.

—vapor is a gas that mixes with air.

What do they have in common, and what makes them different?

W ater, ice, and vapor consist of the same solid small blocks, all identical, called *water molecules*. One cannot see them because they are extremely small: one drop of water contains some billions of billions of molecules!

In fact, a drop of water somewhat resembles a pile of sand in which the grains would be molecules. However, there are many differences:

—First, molecules are so

small that there are as many of them in a drop of water as there exist grains of sand in a mountain 1 kilometer high (0.6 miles)!

—Second, water molecules are somewhat glued to each other: they attract each other and have a tendency to get closer and assemble. Therefore, they form round drops.

—Third, they move! In a drop of water, water molecules are moving constantly, they change place, they slow down, and they speed up. We do not see movement when observing a drop because molecules are very small and very numerous. The situation can be compared to a million people assembled in one place where they keep moving randomly. From a plane at high altitude, one would see a black spot and no movement would be perceived. Well, in a drop of water, not only one million "persons" exist but billions of billions!

Ice and vapor are formed by the same water molecules. The difference is in the way that they move.

In ice, water molecules are well attached to one another. They may vibrate a little in place, but they cannot wander off. This is the reason ice cubes keep their shape: those molecules in a corner of the ice cube cannot leave and form a bump elsewhere.

In contrast, molecules in vapor are entirely free. They are

not even glued to one another as in liquid water. They travel freely, each one its own way, and much more rapidly than do those in liquids. When a vapor molecule hits another, they bounce back. This explains why vapor mixes with air: air is also formed by free molecules (different from those of water) that move in all directions, leaving much space between them. When the air contains water vapor, vapor molecules travel among the others, hitting them from time to time.

In short, the same molecules form ice (when they are firmly attached together), liquid water (when they are close to each other, but not attached), or vapor (when the molecules are far apart from each other). Now, what makes them change from one stage to the other?

The Effect of Heat

The higher the temperature, the greater the movement among the molecules. If an ice cube is heated, its temperature rises. Its molecules cannot move since they are attached to one another. All they can do is vibrate in place at an increasing rate. When the temperature

An ice cube melts when taken out of the refrigerator. Similarly, the lower part of a glacier melts when it reaches the bottom of a valley.

reaches 0°C (32°F), the melting temperature of ice, the molecules can no longer increase their vibration: they must break the "links" that hold them together. Only then can they change place: the ice cube becomes smaller and rounder and water starts to flow. During all the time of melting, the temperature of ice does not increase: heat serves only to separate the molecules.

When all the molecules are loose, only liquid water remains, which consists of closely spaced molecules moving in all directions. If one continues to heat, the temperature rises and the molecules move faster and faster, remaining next to each other, however.

For example, if a pan containing water is heated on the stove, not much happens at first: the molecules move faster and

Without a lid, *vapor escapes into the air of the room. With a lid, most of it assembles in liquid drops.*

faster; however, one cannot see them, even under the microscope, because they are much too small. When the temperature reaches 100°C (212°F), however, large bubbles are formed that rise to the surface and burst, causing agitation everywhere in the water: one says that the water is boiling. Water vapor leaves the pan and mixes with air. As long as water is boiling, its temperature remains at 100°C: all the heat provided is used merely to separate the molecules.

However, if the pan is covered with a lid, and since that lid is a little cooler, vapors cool upon contact with it and the molecules become attached to

each other to form water droplets: the lid is covered with small droplets.

Thus vapor changes back to liquid when cooling: it is said to *condense*. In the same way, the cooling of water can lead to its change into ice.

However, one should notice carefully that during all these adventures, molecules do not change at all: what changes is their freedom of movement.

Why Does Water Evaporate?

Water evaporates (that is, changes into vapor) when it is left on a plate, for instance. After some time the plate is dry, which means that all the water has changed into vapor that has mixed with the air. In the same way, wet laundry dries in a few hours without having been heated at 100°C. Why does water change into vapor without being heated?

Let us first try to understand how a molecule can leave a liquid and disappear in the surrounding air.

In the liquid, all molecules are attracted to each other: a molecule is attracted by all its neighbors. If the molecule is inside the liquid, it is attracted just as much upward or downward, toward the right or the left. However, if it rises to the surface, all its neighbors are located on the same side, namely toward the inside: thus the molecule is attracted toward the inside. To overcome this attraction and to be able to escape, the molecule must acquire momentum: it must reach a rather high speed.

We have previously learned that in the liquid state, molecules move faster with increasing temperature. However, it is temperature that determines

To dry laundry, *it is not necessary to heat it at 100°C (212°F).*

their average speed. This does not mean that all molecules have the same speed. The situation can be compared to a student with a B average at the end of the semester. This does not mean that every test was graded B. He may have had lower and higher grades at times.

Well at 25°C (77°F), for example, water molecules have a certain average speed. Nevertheless, some have a lower and others a higher speed, and since they constantly bump into each other, changes of speed occur all the time. At times, a molecule may surface with sufficient speed to escape the attraction of the others; thus it leaves the water and goes off all by itself into the air.

This is how the fastest molecules leave the water, a situation that decreases the average speed of the others. Similarly, if the two best grades of a student are withdrawn, his yearly average grade decreases! Therefore, the remaining water is slightly cooler than before. The plate and the air of course provide some heat to the water so that it remains at the same temperature as the room. The average speed of the molecules increases again, and some molecules are fast enough to leave in turn—and so on until no water is left on the plate.

The Bowl and the Carafe

Molecules that escape the water continue to move in the air above it. There, they bump into molecules of air and thus bounce in all directions. From time to time, a water molecule falls back into the water and remains there.

Above a bowl, this rarely happens because the molecules have lots of space to escape. However, in a carafe, only those molecules can leave that, by chance, happen to be in the neck of the carafe. Otherwise, they bounce against the walls and have many opportunities to reach the surface of the water and find themselves back in the liquid. Therefore, water in a carafe evaporates much less rapidly than water in a bowl.

And in a closed carafe? Vapor molecules cannot leave, and after a time so many concentrate above the liquid that many return to "glue" themselves to the surface, where they become as numerous as those that are leaving that surface. Therefore,

Water evaporates less rapidly in a carafe, in particular if the carafe is closed!

the number of vapor molecules remains constant as long as the bottle remains shut.

At that time, air in the carafe contains a maximum of water vapor: it is the most humid air possible, at least at this temperature.

Indeed, the maximum amount of water vapor in 1 liter (1 quart) of air depends upon temperature. At 30°C (86°F), 1 liter of air contains at the most 32 milligrams of vapor; at 25°C (77°F), 25 mg; at 20°C (68°F), 19 mg; at 15°C (59°F), 14 mg; at 10°C (50°F), 11 mg; at 5°C (4°F), 8 mg; at 0°C (32°F), 6 mg; at −5°C (22°F), 4 mg; and at −10°C (5°F), 3 mg.

Listen carefully! These figures indicate the maximum amount of water vapor that 1 liter (1 quart) of air can hold at various temperatures. However, this air may hold much more water in the form of liquid droplets, as in fog for example.

But how does one distinguish vapor from liquid? Simply as follows:

WATER VAPOR IS INVISIBLE!

Vapor is a transparent gas like air and is as invisible as air. Therefore, when we can see fog, a cloud, or a plume, it cannot be vapor: these features are necessarily liquid droplets. They can be seen.

The Plume of the Teakettle

When water is boiling in a tea-kettle, a plume rises from the spout and everybody calls this vapor.

However, this is not true: vapor is a transparent gas, as invisible as air. This plume is not invisible, hence it is not vapor! It is a cloud of liquid droplets. Where do they come from?

Even before water begins to boil, the air in the teakettle holds a lot of water vapor, much more than air in a bottle because the teakettle is very hot. It holds, say, 400 milligrams of vapor per liter. As soon as this air full of vapor leaves the spout of the teakettle, it cools and can no longer hold as much vapor. The excess vapor condenses into droplets that are carried upward by the rising hot air. This is the origin of the plume.

And later? Little by little, air coming from the teakettle mixes with air in the room. Once spread over the room, the amount of water is perhaps no longer too large to turn into vapor: the droplets evaporate and disappear.

However, if a teakettle boils

too long, the air in the kitchen is loaded with vapor to its maximum capacity. What happens then? The vapor condenses into droplets, most often on the windowpanes because these are generally colder than the walls. To make these droplets disappear rapidly, one has merely to open the windows. Drier air from the outside mixes with that from the kitchen. Humid air leaves, and soon the air in the kitchen is no longer loaded to its maximum with water vapor. The droplets evaporate and the windowpanes become dry.

There is another way to show that the plume of the teakettle is not vapor. When the water boils rapidly, one can look sideways at the spout of the teakettle and see clearly that the plume starts only shortly after its exit. What actually flows out from the teakettle is very hot transparent water vapor, and it travels a small distance in the air before cooling enough for the first droplets of liquid water to appear. Thus, one realizes that the plume is formed by cooling of what leaves the teakettle.

In cold weather, our breath produces a plume of droplets just as the teakettle does.

Why Is Our Breath Visible in Cold Weather?

The air we breathe out is warm (about 35°C, or 85°F) and loaded with humidity in varying amounts. Suppose that it holds 14 milligrams per liter.

When flowing out, this air cools. If its temperature drops to 18°C (64°F), it can hold only 8 milligrams of vapor. The excess 6 milligrams condenses and produces a cloud of droplets. So you see, the colder the air, the thicker the cloud.

And the real clouds in the sky? They too are formed by droplets of liquid water resulting from the condensation of water vapor, and at times of tiny needles of ice that have the same origin. Indeed, air always holds water vapor, in particular from the evaporation of free water (from oceans, lakes, and rivers), but also from the transpiration and respiration of plants and animals.

When a mass of humid air

rises because it is heated by the sun (the way that a hot-air balloon does), it cools. It would take too long to explain why, but everyone knows that it is cold on top of mountains. It may be that this air is quite humid and it cools enough so that part of the vapor condenses into droplets. Of course, the most important masses of humid air are formed above the ocean and the wind later blows them landward.

If a mass of humid *air rises high enough, it forms clouds.*

Steam

When humid air touches something cold, the water vapor it holds condenses into fine droplets of liquid that cover a cold wall. This is the steam that one sees being formed in summer in a glass of ice water: these droplets do not come from the glass; they come from vapor in the air!

Steam also prevents children from seeing out when their noses are glued against a window. Even if the window is not very cold, the exhaled air is so humid that the window is rapidly covered with steam.

Finally, steam covers car windows when it is cold outside. The breath of the passengers is so humid that soon the air reaches the maximum capacity of humidity with respect to the temperature of the coldest parts of the wall: the car windows. The windshield above the dashboard can of course be heated to remove steam: steam then forms on other car windows where it may be less of a bother. To have steam disappear completely in a car, open the windows: the outside air is drier and when it replaces the air in the car, the steam evaporates.

It may seem strange that outside air is drier even when it is raining. Nevertheless, let us remember that the humidity of air depends only upon vapor. Even if it rains, air at 10°C (50°F) can hold only 11 milligrams of vapor per liter. Once heated in the car, this air is not as humid and no longer loaded to the maximum!

Morning Dew

Dew is steam that forms at night and covers plants. On a clear night without clouds, the earth and all living things on it cool off and radiate infrared. Since leaves radiate well and are not very large with respect to their surface, they cool very rapidly, even faster than the ground itself.

As a matter of fact, air always holds water vapor. When air cools in contact with cold leaves, vapor condenses and forms steam. When vapor is abundant, it assembles in droplets that are found on leaves in the morning. This is morning dew.

When the nights are very cold, this dew is so cold that instead of droplets forming a fine powder of ice or frost is formed. Frost also replaces dew

on the windows in unheated rooms when it is very cold outside. On the inside of windows, a kind of white "flower" —"Jack Frost"—grows that is made of ice layers of various thickness and pattern.

Why Does Alcohol Cool the Skin?

If alcohol is put on the skin (for instance on a wound), a sharp cold is felt at the wet place, if the wound itself does not sting enough to make us forget all the rest. This sensation of cold is caused by evaporation of the alcohol.

Indeed, we have already learned that the fastest molecules escape and that their departure causes a lowering of the liquid's temperature. Well, this cooled liquid is heated in turn by the skin! Immediately thereafter, alcohol continues to evaporate and additional heat must be provided until there is no liquid left. Losing heat gives us a sensation of cold that becomes stronger with increasingly rapid evaporation. This sensation is even stronger with ether than with alcohol because ether evaporates even more rapidly.

The Cooling of Water

To cool water, it is necessary to take away some of its heat. The fastest method of cooling water is to add ice cubes to it. Much heat is required to melt ice, and the water that provides this heat cools very fast: a small ice cube can cool a large glass of water.

If no ice cubes are available, it is possible to remove heat from water by evaporation. For example, in a hot, dry area, such as the southwest, wrap a bottle in a wet cloth: the evaporation of water in the cloth uses heat, part of which comes from the bottle, which cools off nicely, as does the water in the bottle.

Instead of evaporating water in a cloth, a porous container may be used that lets a small amount of water escape very slowly. Evaporation of this water is capable of cooling the portion that remains in the container. This is the method used in the Sahara Desert, where water is carried in goat-skin pouches. Water oozes through the skin and it evaporates very well in this dry, hot climate. The water remaining in the pouch stays deliciously cool.

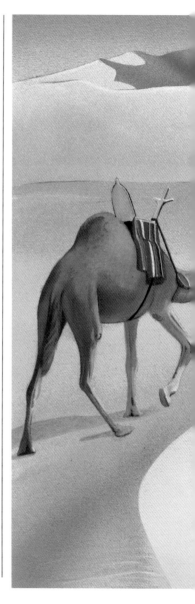

In Greece, the same result is obtained with porous terracotta jars.

Why must air be dry for this method to be effective? The reason is that if the air holds many molecules of vapor, many more would join the liquid water one is trying to evaporate. Therefore, evaporation takes longer—as in the carafe compared with the bowl (see p. 42)—because the air in the carafe was more humid than the air above the bowl.

For the same reason, laundry takes longer to dry when the air is humid. What are the best conditions for drying laundry? Sun and wind at the same time. Indeed, the wind instantly blows away the air that has received humidity from the laundry and replaces it with dry air. Therefore, water molecules have fewer chances to return to the laundry.

For this reason also, one blows on soup to cool it. Soup cools mainly by evaporation: when blowing, water molecules that linger above the surface are chased away and prevented from returning to the liquid to reheat it. Evaporation and hence cooling are thus accelerated.

51

Animal Heat

Heat exchange plays an important role in very many fields, from the evolution of stars to the formation of rocks, going through all the conditions that determine climates (like wind and rain). However, the field closest to us is certainly our bodies. Here, heat and its movements are displayed at every moment—as well as in all other animals, of course—in particular "warm-blooded" animals.

Fish, batrachians (frogs, toads, and tritons),and reptiles (crocodiles, turtles, lizards, and snakes) are often called cold-blooded animals. In reality, their blood is not really cold: it is at the same temperature as the outside. If a fish swims in the North Atlantic, where the water is at 10°C (50°F), its blood is at 10°C. If it swims in equatorial waters at 30°C (86°F), its blood is at 30°C.

In contrast, a warm-blooded animal, that is, a bird or a mammal, lives only if its body is at a very precise temperature.

Humans, for instance, have a normal temperature close to 37°C (98°F). Even if they are very ill, their body temperature cannot vary more than a few degrees from its normal value. Therefore, a warm-blooded animal must keep its body at the same temperature whether it is hot or cold outside.

The same fish *may have cold or warm blood depending upon the temperature of the ocean.*

What Causes Animal Heat?

The heat of firewood is produced by the changing of wood—and of air—into ashes and gases. One must not forget the air, which is as important as the wood.

In the same fashion, animal heat is produced by the changing of food—and of breathed air—into waste products that are eliminated by the body. However, we should not believe that animal heat is produced by the digestion of food. In fact, what produces most heat is the activity of the muscles that "burn" the products made by digestion together with the breathed air carried to the muscles by the blood.

We are warmer when using our muscles instead of remaining still. If I am cold after a long swim, I get warmer much faster by running on the beach instead of remaining still in one place! My body "knows" this very well: when it is cold, what does it do? It shivers, that is, it makes all its muscles work by very small, rapid movements.

Therefore, muscle activity is the most important producer of heat. The whole body takes advantage of this process because blood carries heat very well. However, heat is produced at certain times and not at others, but the body temperature must *always* remain the same. It is therefore necessary that my body lose more heat at certain moments than at others. It can do this in several ways.

First, blood can circulate more or less close to the surface of the skin. When the body must lose heat (when it works particularly hard), it gets very

The two ways of getting warm after a swim.

red because tiny blood vessels just under the skin enlarge so that additional blood can circulate there and cool off at the surface of the body. In contrast, when the body is at rest, it has less heat to lose, and the same blood vessels become very small so that blood cannot circulate too close to the surface. Therefore, the skin is no longer red.

Second, the body loses heat by breathing out warm air, and this is one of the effects of panting caused by an effort (panting serves mainly to bring more air to the muscles).

Finally, and this is the most efficient way, the body loses heat by evaporation of sweat. At the surface of the skin, perspiration evaporates and this evaporation cools the body, just as the evaporation of alcohol did. Of course, perspiration plays other roles as well, but this one is very important. Furthermore, it is not the only liquid that cools the body by evaporation. The air blown by breathing out is full of water vapor that evaporates in particular in the throat and mouth (their dryness signals that the body lacks water and it is time to give it some).

In short, a body that must lose much heat is red, sweating, and panting, the image of an athlete during a workout!

Other warm-blooded animals have the same symptoms. A dog that is hot pants and if it lets its long wet tongue hang out, it is to lose heat by evaporation.

The jerboa, *an expert in water economy.*

Dry Heat, Humid Heat

Whether the evaporation of perspiration provides efficient cooling naturally depends upon the humidity of the air. This is why one can stand heat much better when the air is dry than when it is loaded with moisture. In humid air, just as laundry is difficult to dry, perspiration also does not evaporate well. The skin sweats, the shirt sticks to the back, but since evaporation is lacking, the skin does not cool and the heat is unbearable. The body withstands a temperature of 40°C (104°F) in the Sahara desert much better than a tem-perature of 35°C (95°F) in the equatorial forest.

However, perspiration uses water! In order not to use too much, the inhabitants of the desert cover themselves completely from head to foot, which always seems astonishing.

For the same reason, some desert animals have no perspiration glands at all. Jerboas, for example, are small rodents that leap like kangaroos. They cannot produce sweat, and if a jerboa is suddenly caught by heat outside its hole, it can cool itself only by licking its fur so that it can get some benefit from the evaporation of its saliva for lack of perspiration!

Why Are There No Mice the Size of a Fly?

Warm-blooded animals lose heat at the surface of their bodies. Therefore, they must eat in proportion to that surface.

A small mouse has a skin surface about 500 times smaller than that of a human. It must therefore eat 500 times less. If a human consumes, for instance, 1 kilogram of food per day (2.2 pounds), the mouse eats about 2 grams (0.07 ounces). However, a mouse weighs 10,000 times less than a human, that is, about 8 grams (0.36 ounces). There-fore, it has to eat one-fourth of its weight per day, which means a lot of work!

If warm-blooded animals existed that were no larger than flies, their skin surface would be 100 times smaller than that of a mouse: they would need about 2 centigrams of food (0.00035 ounces) per day. However, their weight would be 8 milligrams! They would therefore have to eat—and digest—three times their weight every day: this is impossible. Therefore, no warm-blooded animals exist that are much smaller than mice.

A field mouse weighs 5 grams (0.175 ounces) in its prime.

The Large Ears of Elephants

Elephants are very large animals. Their tons of muscles must release much heat, and moreover, they live in regions where the climate is rather hot. To lose much heat, a large skin surface is necessary where blood can circulate to cool off. The bodies of elephants are rather heavy and the skin surface is small in comparison to their weight. They would not be able to lose enough heat if they did not have large ears!

Indeed, the ears represent one-fourth of the body surface (let us not forget that skin exists on both sides of the ear) and they are full of small blood vessels. Furthermore, an elephant can move them gently like fans

to move the air around the ears and to cool the blood that circulates in them.

How to Keep Warm in Icy Waters

Water is not a very good conductor of heat; however, like air, it moves and can thus carry heat. It is even more efficient than air in this respect: one cools off much faster in water than in air at the same temperature. Even so, warm-blooded seals spend their lives in icy waters. How do they manage not to lose too much heat?

First of all, their stocky bodies, almost without limbs, have a rather small surface with respect to their weight.

Then, under their skin is a thick layer of fat, an excellent insulator against cold (this is why swimmers who cross large bodies of cold water cover themselves with grease. They don't have enough fat under the skin so they add it on top!)

Finally, seals have an extraordinary blood system. Blood vessels that start in the center of the body (warm) flow toward the surface (cold) and come in contact with blood vessels that flow in the other direction. Thus, blood flowing toward the surface cools in contact with blood that returns, and at the same time, blood from the center warms blood on the surface. Blood arriving at the surface is thus much cooler than it was in the center and loses less heat at the surface. When the "cold" blood returns toward the center, it has enough time to warm up before reaching the vital organs in the middle of the body. In this manner, heat exchanges occur mainly from one part of the blood to the other, thus preventing external losses.

This particular system of blood circulation is called the *rete mirabile* or "wonderful network." A similar system exists in the paws of dogs and allows them to walk all day long "barefoot" in snow!

The Cold That Makes You Blush

A child playing in the snow generally has a red nose and red ears—and also red hands if she was unfortunate enough to have lost her gloves.

Nevertheless, isn't my face normally red when I am hot?

Not necessarily: only when the small blood vessels just under the skin are enlarged. This happens when I am hot and when the body is getting rid of too much heat. However, it may also occur when the body "decides" to sacrifice excess heat to prevent an endangered part from cooling off too much.

In fact, a child playing in the snow is very warm underneath her clothes. Only a very small part of the skin, the face, and in particular, "what sticks out," the nose and the ears, are exposed to the cold. To heat these endangered areas, the body can spend excess heat since it is well protected elsewhere, and hence it enlarges the small blood vessels of the nose and the ears so that warm blood circulates faster in them.

Seals *are warm-blooded, as we are. Nevertheless, they spend their entire lives in icy waters.*

Heat and Humanity

What exactly makes us comfortable? Comfort is when the body achieves its equilibrium easily, when it needs neither to take "drastic actions" to lose heat (redness or perspiration, for example) nor to shiver to resist the cold.

By and large, the body is better equipped to protect itself against heat than cold. Therefore, most people need protection from the cold to be comfortable (that is, prevention of heat loss). Three means exist: clothing, shelter, and heating.

We have already talked about clothing, whose main purpose is to prevent the loss of air warmed by the body. In regard to shelter, particularly houses, things are not so simple.

When searching for the different ways that a house can lose heat, one begins by looking for the means to prevent such losses.

First, the ground on which the house is built is conductive and heat can spread there. To prevent such losses, one must separate the house from the ground by a cellar, for instance (the air of the cellar is a rather good insulator). With respect to these heat losses through the ground, all campers know well that to keep the heat in, it is as important to have a blanket underneath as above.

Drafts are the second cause of heat loss. Of course it is necessary to circulate the air in a

house and it is healthy to sleep in a room with an open window. However, heat losses can be important, especially underneath doors and when windows are open on both sides of the house so that a draft is created.

The third cause of heat loss is through closed windows. Indeed, a windowpane is very thin and heat can easily pass through it. The air in the room cools off against the window. Being cooler, this air sinks and warm air replaces it, which cools off in turn. The exact opposite occurs outside, of course: air heated against the window rises and is replaced by cold air, and so forth.

To prevent such heat loss it is best to have double windows (storm windows or thermopanes). Indeed, the layer of air enclosed between two windows is a very good insulator, and this air is locked in. It may be able to move, of course, but with difficulty. Where winters are very harsh, almost all windows have double panes. Without these, it is possible to hinder air circulation close to the window by installing shutters (outside or inside) or at least by curtains.

Finally, heat escapes through walls. It is thus to our advantage to build well-insulated walls. Hence walls of stone or concrete must be thick; when thin, walls must be built with good insulating material (for instance, double wooden walls). Thick stone walls have an advantage over thin insulated walls in areas of the country that have hot days and very cold nights. Thick walls take a long time to heat during the day (keeping the house cool) and they also take a long time to cool at night when one tries to keep heat inside the house.

All these precautions (thick walls, double windows, and shutters) of course cost more money during construction. For this reason, many houses are built with thin walls and simple windows. Thus home builders save money and those who rent apartments must pay a lot to keep themselves warm, namely by heating.

An Astonishing Solution: the Igloo

In winter, Eskimos live in huts of snow: igloos. In fact, today they no longer live in igloos permanently, they only spend the night there during their

A heat trap that is almost perfect: the igloo.

hunting trips.

An igloo is an ideal shelter against the cold: it is practically impossible for heat to escape!

First, the snow forming the bottom and the walls is an excellent form of insulation (people living in small chalets in the mountains know this well). Furthermore, an igloo has the shape of a half-sphere; that is, it has a small surface with respect to its volume. Since it is the surface that determines the heat loss, this is an ideal shape.

Moreover, the round shape of the walls efficiently reflects toward the center the little heat radiated by an oil lamp and by people themselves.

Replacement of air is provided through a single opening that is also a long tunnel. Finally, people sleep on rather high platforms to benefit from the "warm air" that concentrates under the round roof.

Thus, people have succeeded in these glacial areas where nothing but snow exists in using that snow and living without heating and construction materials!

In a Hot and Dry Area

In hot and dry areas, such as the borders of the Sahara desert, the problem is of course how to protect oneself against heat. Since nights are very cool in these areas—we have learned that nights in the desert can be truly cold—one must mainly prevent the sun from heating the inside of houses in daytime and keep the valuable cool night air gained as long as possible inside. For that reason, traditional desert architecture uses all possible means.

Walls are thick and insulating (dry earth) and often painted white to reflect most of the solar radiation. This does not prevent their cooling by radiation at night because the color of the paint has little influence on infrared radiation.

The outside of a house is generally without windows: sunlit rooms are not desired. Streets are very narrow and often under arcades so that walls are almost always in the shade. Houses have closed courtyards where cold air gathers at night and stays cool all morning. The closed courtyard of Spanish houses was inherited from the Arabs: it is the "patio" that one also finds in South America and in other hot places. A patio is often surrounded by arcades into which all the rooms of the house open and where air circulates well.

A good circulation of air exists throughout the house. It is carefully channeled and directed; indeed, air flows from room to room through holes in floors and ceilings, and there is often a higher room that attracts hot air like a chimney.

Finally, water is made to flow over slabs of stones, and its rapid evaporation in these dry areas provides deliciously cool air.

All these measures represent traditional ways of protection against dry heat. Of course in the large cities of these areas, buildings of steel and glass must be air-conditioned, that is, cooled by refrigerators that use electricity and in turn release heat back into the street.

The Sun Is the Origin of Everything

For personal heat—and for the functioning of machines—people burn wood, coal, oil, and gas and use electricity. Where does all this come from? Almost entirely from solar radiation, that is, from the sun.

The sun is responsible for the growing of plants that provide wood for heat as well as food for all animals (of course, the fox does not eat grass, but without grass there would be no rabbits). By "burning" their food, animals, including humans, live and produce work. One might say that all in all it is the sun that pulls all the weight.

Coal is wood that has been buried for millions of years and has changed over that long period of time. Indeed, it contains imprints of leaves and bark that prove its origin: this wood has grown because of the sun.

Similarly, petroleum originates from animal remains that were first buried on the bottom of the sea and underwent changes during millions of years when former marine deposits were uplifted and became the present continents. Thus, petroleum originates from animals that ate plants—and these plants grew because of the sun!

Two sorts of gas exist that are used for burning: "illuminating gas," made from coal, and natural gas found in the earth the same way petroleum was and for the same reason: they both

have the same origin.

All this from the sun.

How about electricity? It is produced by alternators turning by different means, the most common being the steam engine and the waterfall.

The steam engine uses heat made by the burning of coal or petroleum. Electricity produced in this way is made in coal "power plants." But what made this coal or this petroleum? The sun.

Waterfalls are often produced by means of dams constructed across rivers. There, alternators are turned by the weight of falling water. Such a place is called a hydroelectric power plant. However, what lifted the water whose fall is being used. The sun, when it evaporated the water of the ocean, formed clouds that in turn burst into rain or snow and then gave birth to torrents. This electricity too was made by the sun.

A third way to make an alternator (or dynamo) turn is to use the wind, which turns a propeller called a wind pump or windmill. However, the wind blows because areas of different temperatures occur, which again are caused by the sun!

The only methods to produce electricity independently of solar radiation are the use of:

—the power of tides (but such power plants deteriorate rapidly);

—the heat of the earth (volcanoes and hot springs);

—nuclear energy.

Besides these, all the heat we use, all the energy that gives us light and makes our machines work, comes from the sun.

Solar Energy

We have just learned that almost all the energy that we use derives from solar radiation. Why does one then talk in particular about "solar energy"?

This is the energy that can be drawn directly from solar radiation. In fact petroleum and coal are not inexhaustible, and at the present rate of production, in some tens of years not much will be left. Therefore, people have recently been searching for replacement sources using on the one hand nuclear energy and on the other "new energies," in particular the direct use of solar radiation.

The first trials were oriented toward reaching very high temperatures. For this reason, radiation must be concentrated as is done with a hand lens to set fire to a piece of paper. Instead of using a huge lens, one prefers to concentrate radiation with a mirror.

This is done, for instance, at Odeillo, in the French Pyrenees, with a "solar furnace" that reaches temperatures of several thousand degrees Celsius. Its concave mirror has a surface of 2000 square meters (2,390 square yards). Since it would be very difficult to have it always facing the sun, it is fixed, whereas some sixty smaller plane mirrors, which are movable, reflect radiation toward the larger mirror.

Much smaller mirrors can also be used to grill meat or boil water.

What can be done without concentrating radiation? Without mirrors? Very high temperatures cannot be reached, but water can be heated, for instance to warm houses or to operate special motors for pumping water. In semiarid regions, water often occurs at depth in aquifers. At the same time sun is plentiful to be used for pumping!

In fact, all the systems that use solar energy have the same drawbacks: they work only with the sun. They can be used only in daytime and in very sunny

The solar mirror at Odeillo, a 2000 m² (70,000 ft²) lens

places. Nevertheless, they produce heat without smoke and waste products and are moreover free of charge.

A Marvelous Invention: the Tree

Without using hot water heating, one may take advantage of the sun to heat a house during winter. There are various methods. For instance, air may be circulated between a dark wall (which absorbs radiation well) and a windowpane that the facade of a house facing south has a large surface of windows. In winter, the sun is lower in the sky than in summer and its radiation enters farther into the rooms.

In winter, trees without leaves admit solar radiation.

Of course, this southern facade full of windows may let in too much sun in summer. However, at that time the rays of the sun are almost vertical and enter less. Furthermore, an ideal system exists that lets solar radiation enter in winter and stops it automatically in summer: a tree!

In winter, a bare tree lets the sun enter. In summer, the tree stops the sun and keeps the front of the house shaded! Trees also have many other qualities: they protect against the wind, purify the air, regulate humidity, and shelter birds.

And finally, they are beautiful and contribute to the well-being of people.

In summer, trees covered with leaves provide shade.

Index

Numbers in italics refer to illustrations.

A

Acetylene, 24
Air
   cold, 11, 12, 14, 16,
    18, 20, 46
   currents, 14
   dry, 35, 44, 48, 50, 51
   hot, 12, 14, 16, 17, *18*,
    18, 47
   humid, 43, 44, 45, 46,
    47, *47*, 48
Alcohol, 49
Animals, cold-blooded,
   52, 53
Animals, warm-blooded,
   52, 54, 56, 57, 58, 59,
   60, 61, *60*, *61*, 62, 62

B

Blood vessels, 62
Bowl, 42, *43*
Breath, 46, *46*

C

Carafe, 42, 43, *43*
Chimney, 14, 16, 18
Clothes, 16, *16*, 17
Clouds, 34, 35, 46, 71
Coal, 70, *70*, 73
Coal power plants, *70*
Cold, 62
Condensation, 40, 44,
   46, 47, 48, 49
Conductor of heat, 11

D

Dew, 49, *49*
Dogs, 57, 62
Double window (ther-
   mopane), 66

Drafts, 64–66

E

Electric current, 24, 26,
   27
Electricity, 24, *25–26*,
   26, 27, 71, 73
Elephants, 60, *60*, 61, *61*
Ether, 49

F

Fahrenheit, 8
Field mouse, 59
Fire, 12, 14, 16, 18, *19*,
   20, *21*, 22
Flames, 14, *15*, *18*, 24, 28
Frost, 49

H

Heat
   animal, 52, *52*, 54, *55*,
    56, 57
   dry, 58, 69
   humid, 58
Heating, 64, 66, 69, 70
Hot-air balloon, 12, *13*,
   14
Hothouse, 32, *33*, 34
Houses
   white, 30, *30*
"Hundred Degrees", 7–8
Hydroelectric power
   plant, 71
Hydrogen, 12, 14
Hydrogen balloon, 14

I

Ice, 36–40
Ice cubes, *37*, 38, *39*, 50
Igloo, 66, 67, *67*

Illuminating gas, 70
Indians, *12*
Infrared, see Radiation
Insulator, 11, 16, 17, 31
Iron, 20, *21*, 22–23

J

Jerboa, 58, *58*

L

Lake, 6, *6*, 7
Lamp, 24, *25*, 28
Lava
   color, 24, 26, 27
   temperature, 24, 26,
    27
Leaves, tree, 23, 74, 75,
   75
Light, 20, 22, 24, *25*,
   28–30

M

Metal, 10, 11
Metal spoon, 10
Mice, 59, *59*
Mirror, 28–29, *29*, 30, 31,
   72, 73
Molecules
   air, 38–42, 51
   speed, 37–42
   water, 36–42
Montgolfier, 12
Montgolfière, 12, *13*
Muscles, 54–56

N

Natural gas, 70
Neon tubes, 24
Nights, 32, 34, *34–35*, 35

Nuclear energy, 71, 73

O

Odeillo, *72*, 73

P

Paint, white, 30, *30*
Perspiration, 56, 57, 58
Petroleum, 70, 71, 73
Plants, 32, *33*, 34, 49
Plume, 44, 45, *45*
Power plant, 71, *72*

R

Radiation
   infrared, 22, 24
   of objects, 20, *22*, *23*,
      24

S

Sahara desert, 35, 50,
   50–51, 69
Seals, 61, *62*, 63

Smoke, 11, 12, *12*, 14, 16
Snow, 66, 67
Solar energy, 73–74
"Solar furnace", 73
Solar radiation, 73–74
Steam, 48, 49
Steam engine, 71
Styrofoam, 17
Sun, 20, 22, 24, 30, 32,
   70–71, 73, 74–75
Sweat, 56, 57, 58

T

Teakettle, 44, 45, *45*
Temperature
   body, 52, 54–57
   volcano, 24, 26, 27,
      26–27
   water, 4, 6–7, 8, 40, 43,
      50, 52
Thermometer, 4, 6, 7, 8,
   26
Thermos bottle, 30, 31,
   31, 32
Tree, 74, *74*, 75, *75*

V

Vacuum, 31
Vapor, 36–38, 40–45, 46,
   46, 47–49
Velvet, black, 28–29, *29*
Volcano, 24, 26, 27,
   26–27

W

Walls, 30, 66, 69
Water
   cooling of, 37, 50
   droplet, 36, *36*, 37, 43,
      45, 46
   evaporation, 40–43,
      43, 46, 46, 51
Waterfall, 71
Wind, 51, 71
Windowpane, 28, *28*, 29,
   29, 32, 48
Wood, 10–11, 70
Wooden spoon, 10, *10*

Z

"Zero degree," 7–8

BARRON'S
FOCUS ON SCIENCE Series

This pocket-sized series explores each topic, with exciting texts and lots of sparkling full-color illustrations. (Age 13 & up). Each book: Paperback, index & bibliography, approx. 80 pp., $4\frac{1}{4}'' \times 7\frac{1}{8}''$, $4.95, Can. $6.95. Each book: contains a handy index and bibliography.

Titles include:

THE ATMOSPHERE, *Maury,* ISBN 4213-1

THE ATOM, *Averous,* ISBN 3837-1

BIOLOGY'S BUILDING BLOCKS, *Chevallier-Le Guyader,* ISBN 4212-3

CLIMATES: PAST, PRESENT AND FUTURE, *Tordjman,* ISBN 3838-X

DESTINATION: OUTER SPACE, *Alter,* ISBN 3839-8

DINOSAURS AND OTHER EXTINCT ANIMALS, *Beaufay,* ISBN 3836-3

EARTH AND THE CONQUEST OF SPACE, *Kohler,* ISBN 3831-2

HEAT AND COLD, *Maury,* ISBN 4211-5

HOW THINGS FLY, *Balibar & Maury,* ISBN 4215-8

LIFE AND DEATH OF DINOSAURS, *Chenel,* ISBN 3840-1

THE ORIGIN OF LIFE, *Hagene & Lenay,* ISBN 3841-X

PREHISTORY, *Barloy,* ISBN 3835-5

VOLCANOES, *Kohler,* ISBN 3832-0

WEATHER, *Kohler,* ISBN 3833-9

All prices are in U.S. and Canadian dollars and subject to change without notice. Order from your bookstore, or direct from Barron's by adding 10% for postage & handling (minimum charge $1.50, Canada $2.00). N.Y. residents add sales tax. ISBN prefix: 0-8120

Barron's Educational Series, Inc.
250 Wireless Blvd. • Hauppauge, N.Y. 11788
Call toll-free: 1-800-645-3476, in N.Y.: 1-800-257-5729
In Canada: Georgetown Book Warehouse
34 Armstrong Ave. • Georgetown, Ont. L7G 4R9
Call toll-free: 1-800-668-4336

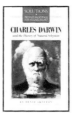
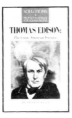